LEARNING ACTIVITIES FOR BUSINESS REPORT WRITING

MARY J. NOBLITT
James Madison University
Harrisonburg, Virginia

JOHN WILEY & SONS
NEW YORK CHICHESTER
BRISBANE TORONTO
SINGAPORE

HF
5719
.N62
1986

Copyright © 1986 by John Wiley & Sons, Inc.

All rights reserved.

Reproduction or translation of any part of this work
beyond that permitted by Sections 107 and 108 of the
1976 United States Copyright Act without the permission
of the copyright owner is unlawful. Requests for
permission or further information should be addressed
to the Permissions Department, John Wiley & Sons.

ISBN   0 471 82931 5

Printed in the United States of America

10 9 8 7 6 5 4 3 2 1

PREFACE

Experiential Learning Activities for Business Report Writing provides students with the opportunity to apply business report writing concepts and principles learned in a report writing or business communication course. A case problem is used throughout the activities to develop different types of reports. These activities are arranged in laboratory format.

Experiential Learning Activities for Business Report Writing can be used with or adapted to any report writing or business communication textbook. Or, they can be used as a source of assignments. These activities are developed for use with electronic office equipment; however, they can also be used in a traditional classroom setting.

These activities adapt well for use in a variety of junior and senior college class configurations. Specific suggestions for using these activities (both in a classroom equipped with electronic media and a traditional classroom) as well as time periods are outlined in the instructor's manual.

ACKNOWLEDGMENTS

The author acknowledges with gratitude the understanding, guidance, and discerning comments given by Dr. John J. Stallard, The University of Tennessee, Knoxville, throughout the planning, and writing of this work. Appreciation is extended to Dr. Betty J. Brown, Ball State University, Muncie, Indiana; Dr. John I. Matthews, The University of Tennessee, Knoxville; and Dr. S. Kyle Reed, The University of Tennessee, Knoxville; for their interest, support, and perceptive observations during the development of these materials.

The author wishes to acknowledge those who carefully evaluated the proposal and reviewed the text. Their comments and suggestions were invaluable:

Delorise Barnes, *Roane State Community College, Oak Ridge, Tennessee*

Raymond W. Beswick, *Hardwick Word Processing Consultants, Ft. McMurray, Alberta, Canada*

Carol Dreger, *Edmonds Community College, Lynwood, Washington*

Doris D. Engerrand, *Georgia College, Milledgeville, Georgia*

Sheila C. Ewing, *Purdue University, Lafayette, Indiana*

Peggy Roberson, *Cuyahoga Community College, Warrensville Township, Ohio*

Gretchen N. Vik, *San Diego State University, San Diego, California*

Acknowledgment is given to Dr. Ross F. Figgins, Consulting Editor for this project; and to Dr. Donald Reese, The University of Tennessee, Knoxville, for his cooperation in testing the materials in his business report writing class.

CONTENTS

INTRODUCTION
    General Objectives   1
    Definition of Terms   3
    Content Outline of Laboratory Sessions   5
    Tips for Using Equipment   7

EXPERIENTIAL LEARNING ACTIVITIES
    Pre-Lab—*Becoming Acquainted With Equipment—
        Activity 1*   11
    Lab I—*Writing an Information Report in Memorandum
        Format—Activities 2-4*   15
    Lab II—*Writing an Introduction—Activities 5-7*   25
    Lab III—*Writing an Introduction (cont'd)—Activity 8*   33
    Lab IV—*Evaluation I*   35
    Lab V—*Developing a Questionnaire—Activity 9*   37
    Lab VI—*Interpreting the Data—Activity 10*   43
    Lab VII—*Evaluation II*   57
    Lab VIII—*Stating Findings, Deriving Conclusions, and
        Making Recommendations—Activities 11-14*   59
Lab IX—*Evaluation III*   69
Lab X—*Writing a Letter Report—Activity 15*   71

REFERENCE GUIDE   73

LEARNING ACTIVITIES FOR BUSINESS REPORT WRITING

INTRODUCTION

These experiential learning activities are designed to provide you with practice activities which will reinforce the report writing concepts you have learned in the lecture session prior to laboratory application. A case problem is used throughout the activities. You will use the same topic and build on each type of report to develop the next one. Concurrently with the practice activities, you will be completing your _final_ report.

All laboratory activities are _practice_ except Labs IV, VII, and IX. These three labs are designated for evaluation of the work you have completed on the final report. As you complete the practice activities, your instructor will peruse your work as it is displayed on your computer screen and give you instant feedback on it.

It is assumed that by enrolling in the business report writing course you possess the basic English skills in grammar, spelling, punctuation, and syntax. The materials included with these activities will enable you to practice producing documents on electronic communication media. The intent of these activities is not to train you to become a skilled word processor but to help you use technology as a tool of communication.

GENERAL OBJECTIVES

The general objectives of the experiential learning activities are as follows:

1. To become acquainted with the equipment and the concept of interfacing report writing with technology.

2. To complete a reference chart for use with your computer by defining the terms and identifying the function keys to be used.

3. To write an information report in memorandum format.

4. To develop the nine concepts in planning a report. The steps are:

   a. Defining the Problem

   b. Identifying the Reader

   c. Identifying the Essential Factors to be Investigated

   d. Defining the Elements of the Problem

   e. Stating the Purpose(s)

   f. Defining Key Terms (if needed)

   g. Establishing Procedures--Deciding Where and How to Obtain Data

   h. Considering the Scope and Limitations

   i. Presenting Background Information

5. To determine secondary sources of information.

6. To develop a questionnaire.

7. To write an information report.

8. To interpret the primary data collected.

9. To determine the correct use of headings and sub-headings.

10. To use and construct tables, charts, and graphs.

11. To integrate tables, charts, and graphs with the text.

12. To state findings, derive conclusions, and make recommendations.

13. To prepare the prefatory parts of the report:

    a. Title Page

    b. Letter of Transmittal

c. Table of Contents

d. List of Tables

e. List of Figures

14. To prepare the supplemental parts of the report:

    a. Bibliography

    b. Appendices

15. To write an analtyical report.

16. To write a letter report.

DEFINITION OF TERMS

The following are definitions of terms which are used in these experiential learning activities:

1. <u>Analytical Report</u>. An analytical report presents the facts about the problem, analyzes and interprets the data, derives conclusions from the data, and may make recommendations.

2. <u>Concept</u>. A concept is a key idea, topic, or main thought in the subject content of the report writing course.

3. <u>DOS</u>. DOS is the disk operating system that enables the computer to input and output information from disks.

4. <u>Examination Report</u>. An examination report presents the facts about the problem, analyzes these facts about the problem, and interprets the data.

5. <u>Experiential Learning</u>. Experiential learning refers to instructional situations in which primary emphasis is placed on personal experience and in which action exercises are provided in which individuals can test their newly learned theories and concepts.

6. <u>Final Report</u>. The final report is one assigned in the lecture sessions for which the topic is chosen by the class, the questionnaire is developed in class, and the students collect the data from both primary and secondary sources and write the report.

7. <u>Formatting a Disk</u>. Formatting a disk is the process of preparing a blank disk for use with your software.

8. <u>Information Report</u>. An information report presents facts about the problem. The information report has no interpretation of data and no conclusions derived.

9. <u>Practice Report</u>. A practice report is one in which the report writers are provided all the raw data, and they apply the theories learned in lecture sessions to experiential learning activities in a laboratory setting.

10. <u>Primary Source</u>. A primary source is first-hand information gathered and determined by the researcher. The information may be collected by interviews, questionnaires, observations, or experimentation.

11. <u>Secondary Source</u>. A secondary source is one which reflects the experience of others. Examples are books, magazines and periodicals, government documents, reports, bulletins, and brochures.

12. <u>Systems Approach</u>. The systems approach is the integration of all the functions of the activities into an operational system.

13. <u>Technology</u>. Technology refers to the automated equipment in modern offices used for creating, inputting, storing, retrieving, editing, and printing text.

CONTENT OUTLINE OF LABORATORY SESSIONS

Session	Content
<u>Pre-lab</u>	Interfacing Report Writing with Modern Office Technology
	Building a Reference Chart by Completing a Matrix
Lab I	Writing an Information Report in Memorandum Format
Labs II-III	Writing the Introduction by
	a. Stating the problem clearly
	b. Identifying the essential factors to be investigated
	c. Determining the elements of the problem
	d. Stating the purpose(s)
	e. Defining key terms (if needed)
	f. Establishing procedures--deciding where and how to obtain data
	g. Considering the scope and limitations
	h. Presenting the background information
	i. Using headings and subheadings
Lab IV	Evaluation I--Write an information report on the topic decided upon in class. Use factual, impersonal language. The report should include all of the concepts listed in Labs II-III above.

Labs V-VI   Developing a Questionnaire

                 Interpreting Data

                 Constructing Tables, Charts, and Graphs and
                 Integrating Them With the Text

Lab VII   Evaluation II--Write an examination report
                 on the topic decided upon in class. Use the
                 data collected from the questionnaire devel-
                 oped in class. This report should develop
                 all the elements of the problem identified
                 in the information report developed in Lab
                 IV.

Lab VIII   Stating the Findings, Deriving Conclusions,
                 and Making Recommendations

                 Preparing the Prefatory Pages

                 Preparing the Supplemental Pages

Lab IX   Evaluation III--Write an analytical report
                 on the topic decided upon in class. Include
                 the following:

                 a. The information report written in Lab
                    IV.

                 b. The examination report written in Lab
                    VII.

                 c. Findings, conclusions, and recommenda-
                    tions (if used).

                 d. All prefatory and supplemental pages.

Lab X   Write a Letter Report Using the Data Com-
                 piled in the Pratice Report

TIPS FOR USING EQUIPMENT

ALWAYS turn machine on <u>before</u> placing disks in disk drive.

ALWAYS remove disks from drives <u>before</u> turning machine off.

ALWAYS use a felt-tip pen when writing on the disk labels.

ALWAYS handle the disks with care and store properly.

ALWAYS use the arrow keys for revising or editing.

ALWAYS save your document before removing the disks from the drives.

ALWAYS wait until red light is off <u>before</u> removing disks from drives.

ALWAYS return <u>only</u> at the end of a paragraph.

EXPERIENTIAL LEARNING ACTIVITIES

PRE-LAB

ACTIVITY 1

Objectives

    To become acquainted with the equipment.

    To complete a matrix showing the functions and keys to use for the various applications used in the laboratory activities.

    Hands-on introduction to equipment.

Instructions

    I. Complete the matrix (pages 113-127) to use as a reference guide as needed while you are completing the laboratory activities.

    II. Introduction to Equipment

        A. CRT Screen

            1. On/Off Switch

            2. Reset Button

            3. Brightness Control

        B. Keyboards

            1. Typewriter

            2. Ten-key Pad

        C. Disk Drives

            1. Left/Top

            2. Right/Bottom

D. Inserting Disks

   1. Turn System on

   2. Insert DOS disk into appropriate drive and close the disk drive door

   3. Insert data disk into appropriate drive and close the disk drive door

E. Booting/Loading the System--follow instructions for your particular equipment

F. Formatting a Disk--follow equipment instructions for preparing a blank disk for use. When the formatting process is complete, a message will be displayed on the screen telling you that the formatting is finished and whether your disk has any flawed sectors or tracks.

G. If there are no flawed sectors or tracks, the disk is ready for use. To use it follow instructions for your software.

III. Work on a Document File

   A. Place your disks in appropriate disk drives.

   B. Open a document.

   C. Type a name for your document. You must use a disk drive letter or number to tell the system that your document is to be recorded on the data disk.

   D. Follow your software instructions for formatting a document.

   E. Type **Paragraph A** shown below. Center the heading on the line. **RETURN** three times. **Do not** return except at the end of the paragraph. Make corrections as you type.

PARAGRAPH A

       In today's business environment there is an increased awareness of the importance of accurate and effective communication. This awareness is stimulating elaborate procedures and policies to improve the flow and quality of messages in companies. Many businesses are investing in sophisticated electronic communication media to transmit written as well as spoken messages.

F. Return to the beginning of the document. Use the cursor keys to move from line to line and proofread it. Follow correction techniques for your software and correct any errors you find.

G. **SAVE** the document.

LAB I

ACTIVITIES 2-4

Objective

To write an information report in memorandum format.

Concept(s) Prerequisite to Lab I

Identifying the Content of an Information Report

Using Memorandum Format for Writing Reports

LAB 2

ACTIVITIES 2-4

Objective

To write an information report in memorandum format.

Concepts/Skills/Tasks to Lab 2

Identifying the Content of an Information Report

Using Memorandum Format for Writing Reports

ACTIVITY 2

Instructions

Write a one- to two-page information report introducing yourself to the instructor. The report should include such information as your major area of study, your classification, hours completed, career expectations, interests, and extracurricular activities. Use memorandum format.

```
    DATE:
      TO:
    FROM:
 SUBJECT:
```

1. Open a document. Be sure you indicate that you will be working on your data disk.

2. Type document name: **ACT2**.

3. Give the computer any necessary instructions at this time to get you into the open document. Use single spacing and blocked paragraphs.

4. Make any format adjustments necessary.

5. Type the document (report). Make corrections as you type.

6. Proofread the document. Correct any errors you find.

7. **SAVE** the document.

ACTIVITY 3

<u>Instructions</u>

1. Retrieve the document saved in Activity 2.

2. Make the following revisions in the document:

   a. Indent paragraphs 5 spaces.

   b. Change to double spacing.

   c. Reformat the entire document to make the line endings as even as possible by hyphenating where appropriate.

3. **SAVE** the document.

ACTIVITY 4

Instructions

1. **PRINT** the document saved in Activity 3.

2. Go to a work station with a printer. Prepare the printer for use.

   a. Turn printer on.

   b. Insert paper.

3. Boot system to use computer.

4. Retrieve your document: **ACT2**.

5. Follow the necessary steps to print the document on two pages, pausing between pages to remove the first page and to insert the second.

6. Hand in printed document.

Assignment for Lab II

1. Review lecture notes and textbook assignment on writing an introduction.

2. Select two references from the bibliography shown below. Go to the library and read the articles. Be prepared to use the information when revising the introductory section of your **practice** report.

BIBLIOGRAPHY

Randall, James D. "Credit Cards: Effects on Today's
     Consumer Credit Industry," THE CREDIT WORLD, (Aug.-
     Sept. 1979), pp. 22-25.

"Scrambling for Credit," NEWSWEEK ON CAMPUS, (April
     1985), pp. 16-17.

Thornhill, William T. "Credit Cards, A Time for Changes,"
     THE CREDIT WORLD, Vol. 68, No. 5 (April-May 1980),
     pp. 14-18.

Thornhill, William T. "Credit Cards, A Time for Changes,
     Part II," THE CREDIT WORLD, Vol. 68, No. 6 (June-
     July 1980), pp. 8-12.

LAB II
ACTIVITIES 5-7

<u>Objective</u>

    To write an introduction.

<u>Concept(s) Prerequisite to Lab II</u>

1. Gearing the Report to the Reader
2. Defining the Problem
   a. Presenting background information
   b. Stating the problem
   c. Identifying essential factors about the problem to be investigated
   d. Determining the elements (factors) of the problem
3. Stating the Purpose(s)
4. Defining Key Terms
5. Deciding on the Sources of Data - Primary and Secondary
6. Establishing a Method of Procedure
7. Considering the Scope
8. Defining the Limitations
9. Using Headings and Subheadings

Special Instructions

Read the following case carefully. It will serve as a reference base for completing all the practice activities for Labs II - X. Prepare the practice report by following the instructions given in the lab assignments.

CASE

Credit cards have been in use since 1914. However, major innovations in this field did not occur until the 1950s. The use of the credit card has expanded to the point that the wallet has become a repository for such cards rather than for money. College students use credit cards to buy textbooks and supplies, to pay tuition, to buy gas, to travel, in restaurants, and in many other ways. Most companies supplied these cards free of charge until about 1977. Now, many organizations are charging a membership fee of $20 to $45 annually for the use of the card. The rates charged for carrying these accounts have risen, and many states have passed legislation allowing companies to raise finance charges to as much as 24 percent annually.

ACTIVITY 5

Instructions

1. Retrieve the document which is stored on your data disk as **ACT5**.

2. Study the statement of the problem as it is written and revise it.

3. Keep the reader(s) in mind as you define the problem. This includes:

    a. Preparing the reader for what is to come by presenting background information about the problem (Use the information gathered from your outside reading assignment to complete this section of the report.),

    b. Stating the problem,

    c. Identifying and discussing the essential factors to be investigated, and

    d. Determining the elements of the problem.

4. Proofread the document and make any necessary corrections.

5. **SAVE** the document.

ACTIVITY 6

<u>Instructions</u>

1. Retrieve the document stored on your data disk as **ACT6**.

2. Revise the purpose(s) of the report to further define your problem statement.

3. Proofread your document and make any necessary corrections.

4. **SAVE** the document.

ACTIVITY 7

Instructions

1. Open a document on your data disk using the name **ACT7**.

2. Format your document for double spacing and a five-space paragraph indention.

3. Type:

    a. an explanation of data sources to be used to get the needed information to solve the stated problem.

    b. an explanation of the method of procedure to be followed in presenting the data collected.

    c. an explanation of the scope and limitations of the research.

4. Proofread the document and make any necessary corrections.

5. **SAVE** the document.

Assignment for Lab III

1. Continue developing the concepts in writing the introduction.

2. Review lecture notes and textbook assignments on writing the introduction and specifically the use of headings and subheadings.

LAB III

ACTIVITY 8

Objectives

To merge Activities 5-7 into an introduction to the report. (This will also become an information report.)

To use the **appropriate** headings and subheadings.

Concepts Prerequisite to Lab III

1. Using Headings and Subheadings

2. Writing an Introduction

3. Defining an Information Report

Instructions

1. Open a document on your data disk using the name **ACT8**.

2. Make any format adjustments necessary (such as margin stops and line spacing).

3. Type the heading **INTRODUCTION** in all capital letters and centered. Triple space.

4. Merge Activity 5 at this point.

5. Insert side headings where appropriate. Triple space before and double space after the side heading.

6. Underscore the side headings typed using initial capital letters.

7. Merge Activity 6. Follow the instructions for merging Activity 3.

8. Merge Activity 7. Follow the instructions for merging Activity 6.

7. **SAVE** the document.

8. **PRINT** the document.

9. Hand in the completed report.

<u>Assignment for Lab IV</u>

1. Have the introduction to your **final** report ready to type. This will be your first evaluation lab and will represent an important part of your final grade.

2. Review your lecture notes and textbook assignments on the concepts covered to this point.

LAB IV

EVALUATION I

<u>Objective</u>

To write an information report.

<u>Instructions</u>

1. Open a document: **EVAL1**. Be sure to indicate that you will be working on your data disk.

2. Using factual, impersonal language, and the topic selected for your **final** report, write an information report.

3. Include the following topics:

   a. Introduction (include background information, problem statement, essential factors about the problem, and elements of the problem)

   b. Statement of Purpose(s)

   c. Definition of Key Terms (if needed)

   d. Source of Data and Method of Procedure

   e. Scope and Limitations

4. Use Appropriate Headings and Subheadings

5. Follow Format Used in Practice Report

6. **SAVE** the Document

7. **PRINT** the Document

8. Submit the Document for Evaluation

Assignment for Lab V

Review lecture notes and textbook assignments on identifying primary sources of data and questionnaire development.

LAB V

ACTIVITY 9

Objective

To develop a questionnaire.

Concept(s) Prerequisite to Lab V

Determining the Source of Data - Questionnaire

Instructions

1. Retrieve from your data disk the document named **ACT9**.

2. Refer to the elements of the problem in your **practice** report, and revise the questionnaire in this document.

3. Follow the "Guidelines for Developing a Questionnaire" shown on the following page.

4. **SAVE** the document.

5. **PRINT** the document.

Assignment for Lab VI

1. Review lecture notes and textbook assignments on interpreting data and using and constructing tables, charts, and graphs.

2. Review the lab materials (tables, charts, graphs, questionnaire, and tally sheet) and be prepared to type the interpretation section of your **practice** report.

3. Select only those tables, charts, and graphs needed to answer the questions asked in the elements of the problem in your introduction section of the report.

GUIDELINES FOR DEVELOPING A QUESTIONNAIRE

The following is a suggested list of guidelines for developing a questionnaire:

1. Arrange the questions in a logical order. Group related questions together.

2. Make recording, classifying, and analyzing the answers easy. Provide alternative answers which the respondent can circle or check.

3. State each question carefully and address only one topic in each.

4. Do not ask leading questions.

5. Avoid skip-and-jump questions and <u>extensive</u> use of ranking questions.

6. If open-ended questions are used, make them specific.

7. Include an introduction and clear, concise instructions for completing the questionnaire.

8. Limit the length of the questionnaire to no more than two pages.

9. Ask only those questions that are necessary for solving your problem.

10. Write a variety of questions. Include the following kinds:

    a. Yes - No   d. Checklist
    b. Demographic Data   e. Open-ended
    c. Rank Order   f. Rating Scale
              g. Multiple Choice

SAMPLE QUESTIONNIARE

(To be used with Lab V, Activity 9. This questionnaire is also stored on your data disk as **ACT9**)

CREDIT CARDS

A survey of the use of credit cards by (fill in the name of your school) students is being conducted by (class name and number). Your cooperation in completing this questionnaire will be appreciated.

CREDIT CARD: Any card that authorizes a credit purchase such as oil company cards, bank cards, and retail department store charge accounts is classified as a credit card.

PLEASE ANSWER THE FOLLOWING QUESTIONS BY PLACING A CHECK MARK IN THE APPROPRIATE BLANK.

1. What is your age?

    _____ a. 17 or less
    _____ b. 18-20
    _____ c. 21-23
    _____ d. 24-26
    _____ e. 27 or older

2. What is your sex?

    _____ a. Male
    _____ b. Female

3. What is your classification?

    _____ a. Freshman
    _____ b. Sophomore
    _____ c. Junior
    _____ d. Senior
    _____ e. Graduate
    _____ f. Other, list _____

4. What is your marital status?

    _____ a. Single
    _____ b. Married
    _____ c. Other

5. What is your race?

    _____ a. Caucasian
    _____ b. Negro
    _____ c. Oriental
    _____ d. Other, list _____

6. What is the source of your income?

    _____ a. Personal Job
    _____ b. G. I. Bill
    _____ c. Parents
    _____ d. Loan
    _____ e. Other, list _____

7. What is your total monthly income?

    _____ a. $0
    _____ b. Less than $100
    _____ c. $101 - $200
    _____ d. $201 - $300
    _____ e. $301 - $400
    _____ f. $401 or more

8. Do you possess a credit card?

    _____ a. Yes
    _____ b. No

IF YOUR ANSWER TO QUESTION 8 IS <u>NO</u>, PLEASE OMIT THE REST OF THE QUESTIONS.

9. How many cards do you possess?

    _____ a. 1 - 3
    _____ b. 4 - 6
    _____ c. 7 - 9
    _____ d. 10 or more

10. What type of credit cards do you have? (Check one or more.)

 _____ a. Oil company cards
 _____ b. Bank cards
 _____ c. Retail department store cards
 _____ d. Other, list _____

11. Where do you use your credit cards? (Check one or more.)

 _____ a. Department stores
 _____ b. Service stations
 _____ c. Restaurants
 _____ d. School tuition
 _____ e. School supplies stores
 _____ f. Beauty shop or barber shop
 _____ g. Government payments
 _____ h. Grocery stores
 _____ i. Motels/Hotels
 _____ j. Others, list _____

12. How often do you use your credit cards monthly?

 _____ a. Never
 _____ b. 1 - 5 times
 _____ c. 6 - 10 times
 _____ d. 11 or more times

13. How do credit cards influence your spending as opposed to paying cash?

 _____ a. Tend to spend more
 _____ b. Tend to spend less
 _____ c. Tend to spend about the same

14. What are the approximate charges on all your credit cards by you and all members of your family in an average month?

 _____ a. $0 - $20
 _____ b. $21 - $40
 _____ c. $41 - $60
 _____ d. $61 - $80
 _____ e. $81 or more

15. What amount do you have charged to your bank or all-purpose credit cards?

   _____ a.   Less than $100
   _____ b. $100 - $200
   _____ c. $201 - $300
   _____ d. $301 - $400
   _____ e.   Other, list _____

LAB VI

ACTIVITY 10

Objectives

1. To select and interpret relevant information from the primary data collected.

2. To use tables, charts, and graphs with the text.

3. To integrate the tables, charts, and graphs with the text.

Concept(s) Prerequisite to Lab VI

1. Interpreting the Data

2. Using and Constructing Tables, Charts, and Graphs

3. Integrating Tables, Charts, and Graphs with the Text

Instructions

1. Open a document on your data disk using the name **ACT10**.

2. Materials needed for the completion of the above objectives are on the pages 67-87.

3. Use the tally of data obtained from completed questionnaire, and selected tables, charts, and graphs to answer the questions listed in the "Factors (Elements) of the Problem" section of this report. (See Lab II, Activity 5).

4. Include only relevant information. Select only those tables, charts, and graphs needed to make your message accomplish its purpose. You may not need to use all of those provided.

5. If you wish, you may use the information provided on tally of data sheets and prepare additional graphs, tables, etc.

6. You will need to use appropriate titles and table and figure numbers for those selected as a part of your practice report.

7. **SAVE** the document.

8. Open a document on your data disk named **ACT10.1**.

9. Merge **ACT8** and **ACT10**.

10. **SAVE** the document.

11. **PRINT** the document.

Assignment for Lab VII

Review all concepts covered to this point. Lab VII will be used to complete the interpretation section of your **final** report. You should be ready to type the informaion integrating your graphs and charts when you get to the lab session. This will be your second evaluation and will represent an important part of your final grade.

TALLY OF RESPONSES TO THE SURVEY ON THE USE OF CREDIT CARDS BY
(NAME OF YOUR SCHOOL), STUDENTS, SPRING 198-

Respondent No.	Question No.														
	1	2	3	4	5	6	7	8	9	10	11	12	13	14	15
1	C	A	D	B	A	A	C	A	A	B	J	A	C	A	A
2	E	A	C	B	A	AB	E	B	–	–	–	–	–	–	–
3	E	A	D	A	A	AB	D	A	A	AC	J	A	C	A	E
4	E	A	D	A	A	BC	C	B	–	–	–	–	–	–	–
5	B	A	C	A	A	AD	A	A	A	B	BJ	B	C	B	B
6	C	A	D	A	B	AC	B	A	A	A	BI	B	C	A	A
7	E	B	E	B	A	ED	A	A	A	C	A	B	C	A	–
8	C	A	D	A	–	A	C	A	A	A	BI	B	C	A	–
9	C	B	D	C	A	CA	B	B	–	–	–	–	–	–	–
10	C	B	D	A	A	CC	B	B	–	–	–	–	–	–	–
11	B	B	C	A	A	CB	A	A	A	AC	ABCI	B	C	E	A
12	D	B	E	A	A	AE	A	B	B	AC	AB	B	C	D	A
13	C	A	D	B	A	C	–	A	A	A	B	B	C	B	–
14	E	A	D	B	A	AE	–	A	A	B	ABDE	B	C	B	B
15	B	B	D	A	B	A	–	B	–	–	–	–	–	–	–
16	B	B	B	B	B	E	–	A	A	C	A	A	C	A	A
17	C	A	D	A	A	A	–	A	A	AB	AB	C	C	C	A

TALLY (Continued)

Respondent No.	1	2	3	4	5	6	7	8	9	10	11	12	13	14	15
18	B	A	D	C	A	AC	–	A	A	ABC	AB	C	A	B	B
19	D	A	C	A	A	AB	C	A	A	B	A	A	B	A	A
20	C	A	D	A	A	AB	B	A	A	AB	BI	B	C	A	B
21	B	A	A	A	A	AC	A	A	A	A	BI	C	C	D	–
22	E	A	D	B	B	AE	F	A	D	ABC	ABCE	C	A	C	E
23	E	A	C	B	B	AE	F	B	B	AB	ABE	C	A	B	A
24	B	A	A	A	A	AC	A	B	–	–	–	–	–	–	–
25	D	A	B	B	B	AB	D	A	B	ABC	AB	B	C	B	D
26	C	A	D	B	B	A	F	A	A	AB	ABCE	D	A	E	D
27	D	A	D	B	B	AE	F	A	C	C	ABC	B	A	A	C
28	E	A	D	A	A	A	D	A	B	ABC	ABEI	C	C	A	C
29	D	A	C	B	B	AB	F	A	–	ABC	ABCD	C	B	E	A
30	E	A	D	B	B	AB	D	B	A	–	–	–	–	–	–
31	E	A	C	B	A	A	F	A	A	AD	BI	B	C	A	A
32	C	A	D	A	A	C	D	A	A	A	BI	C	C	A	E
33	C	B	D	B	A	E	F	A	B	AC	AB	D	A	A	B
34	C	A	C	A	A	AB	E	B	–	–	–	–	–	–	–
35	B	B	B	A	A	C	B	A	A	C	A	A	A	C	A
36	D	A	D	B	A	BC	F	A	B	ABC	ABI	C	A	B	B
37	B	B	A	A	A	E	F	A	A	A	AB	C	C	E	A
38	E	A	E	B	A	A	F	A	C	ABC	ACI	D	C	E	E

TALLY (Continued)

Respondent No.	Question No.														
	1	2	3	4	5	6	7	8	9	10	11	12	13	14	15
39	E	A	D	B	A	E	F	A	A	AC	AB	B	A	B	–
40	D	B	A	B	A	A	E	A	A	C	A	B	A	B	B
41	B	B	A	A	A	A	C	B	–	–	–	–	–	–	–
42	C	A	C	B	A	E	D	B	–	–	–	–	–	–	–
43	D	A	D	A	A	A	F	A	A	AC	ABI	D	A	E	A
44	C	B	E	C	A	A	F	A	A	A	AB	B	C	C	B
45	C	A	D	D	A	A	E	A	A	ABC	BI	C	C	B	A
46	E	A	F	B	A	A	C	A	D	ABC	ADE	C	C	D	B
47	C	B	E	C	A	A	E	A	C	ABC	AB	C	A	E	D
48	E	B	A	A	A	A	F	A	B	ABC	ABI	D	A	D	B
49	C	A	D	A	A	C	B	B	–	–	–	–	–	–	–
50	D	B	E	A	A	E	D	A	A	ABC	AB	B	A	C	A
51	D	B	E	C	B	A	D	A	A	ABC	AB	B	A	C	E
52	D	A	D	B	A	B	F	A	A	A	B	A	C	A	A
53	E	A	D	B	A	A	F	B	ABC	ABC	B	C	C	A	A
54	B	B	D	A	A	C	A	A	A	AD	BJ	B	A	B	A
55	C	B	D	A	A	C	C	A	A	C	A	C	A	E	–
56	C	A	D	A	A	A	C	A	A	A	B	A	A	B	–
57	D	A	D	B	A	AB	F	A	B	ABC	ABCI	D	A	B	B
58	D	A	D	B	A	A	F	A	D	ABC	ABCE	C	C	E	A
59	C	A	D	B	A	E	E	A	A	B	BCI	B	A	A	A
60	C	A	D	B	A	C	E	A	A	A	BC	B	C	B	–
61	C	A	D	A	A	C	D	A	A	A	B	B	B	–	–

47

48

TALLY (Continued)

Respondent No.	\multicolumn{15}{c}{Question No.}
	1	2	3	4	5	6	7	8	9	10	11	12	13	14	15
62	C	A	D	A	A	C	B	B	-	-	-	-	-	-	-
63	C	A	D	A	A	C	B	A	B	A	B	B	C	B	A
64	F	A	D	B	A	A	B	A	D	ABC	ABC	D	C	D	B
65	D	A	D	B	A	A	F	A	B	ABC	AB	B	C	B	A
66	C	A	D	A	A	A	F	A	A	B	BI	C	C	B	A
67	E	B	E	A	A	F	D	B	B	C	ABE	C	C	D	E
68	C	B	D	B	A	A	A	A	B	-	BI	B	C	B	A
69	B	B	C	A	A	A	C	B	B	A	AB	B	A	A	A
70	B	B	E	B	A	A	D	A	A	BC	ABI	B	C	A	A
71	C	B	C	A	A	C	-	A	D	-	B	C	A	B	A
72	C	B	D	A	A	C	A	A	A	BC	ABI	B	C	B	A
73	D	B	E	A	A	A	F	A	C	ABC	ABF	D	A	E	C
74	A	B	B	A	A	C	D	A	A	AB	ABF	B	A	E	A
75	C	A	B	A	A	E	D	A	A	B	B	B	C	E	A
76	C	A	D	A	E	D	D	A	A	A	BCI	A	C	D	A
77	C	A	D	A	A	C	C	A	B	A	CI	B	A	D	C
78	C	A	F	A	A	A	F	A	A	AB	ABCH	B	A	A	-
79	C	B	D	B	A	C	B	A	C	C	A	C	A	B	B
80	C	B	D	B	A	E	C	A	A	ABC	ABCI	B	C	B	A
81	B	B	D	A	A	C	C	A	A	AB	B	B	C	-	-
82	B	B	D	A	A	C	B	A	A	A	B	B	C	B	-
83	D	A	F	A	A	B	C	B	-	-	-	-	-	-	-

TALLY (Continued)

Respondent No.	1	2	3	4	5	6	7	8	9	10	11	12	13	14	15
84	E	B	D	B	A	E	E	A	B	ABC	ABI	D	C	C	C
85	C	B	D	A	A	C	C	A	A	A	B	B	A	A	–
86	B	A	B	A	A	C	D	A	A	ABC	ABCI	D	C	E	A
87	C	B	A	A	C	B	B	–	–	–	–	–	–	–	–
88	C	B	D	A	A	C	B	A	A	C	A	B	C	C	B
89	B	B	C	B	A	A	E	A	A	AC	AB	B	C	A	A
90	C	B	D	A	C	C	A	A	A	C	B	A	C	B	A
91	C	B	D	A	A	C	A	B	–	–	–	–	–	–	–
92	B	B	A	A	A	C	B	B	–	–	–	–	–	–	–
93	B	B	D	B	A	CE	A	A	A	AC	AB	B	A	A	A
94	C	B	D	B	A	E	F	A	C	ABC	ABE	D	C	B	A
95	C	B	D	B	A	E	F	A	B	ABC	ABEI	D	C	B	A
96	C	B	D	A	A	AB	D	B	B	ABC	AB	B	C	B	B
97	C	A	E	B	A	AC	B	A	A	–	–	–	–	–	–
98	C	A	D	B	A	CE	C	A	A	D	CI	B	C	A	A
99	C	A	D	B	A	CE	F	A	A	A	BA	B	C	E	E
100	C	A	D	B	A	AC	D	A	B	BC	ABC	C	C	D	A
101	C	A	D	B	A	AC	E	A	A	ABC	B	A	C	A	E
102	C	A	D	A	A	AC	A	A	A	ABC	ABI	C	C	E	B
103	B	A	D	A	A	C	A	A	A	A	B	B	C	E	A
104	D	A	D	B	A	A	F	B	–	–	–	–	–	–	–
105	C	B	D	C	A	C	A	A	A	AB	AB	C	B	E	B

TALLY (Continued)

Respondent No.	1	2	3	4	5	6	7	8	9	10	11	12	13	14	15
106	C	B	F	B	A	A	F	B	–	–	–	–	–	–	–
107	D	B	E	B	A	E	F	A	A	CD	ACI	C	C	C	D
108	B	B	D	B	A	E	A	A	A	C	A	B	C	A	E
109	C	A	D	B	A	C	F	A	A	A	BI	D	C	B	–
110	B	B	C	A	A	C	C	B	–	–	–	–	–	–	–
111	C	A	C	A	A	C	C	A	A	A	BI	C	C	E	A
112	B	A	C	A	A	C	A	A	B	AB	AB	B	C	–	A
113	C	A	D	B	C	C	A	A	A	A	B	B	A	B	E
114	A	A	B	A	A	E	A	B	–	–	–	–	–	–	–
115	C	B	D	B	A	C	A	A	A	A	B	A	C	A	A
116	B	B	B	A	A	E	C	A	A	AB	AB	B	C	A	–
117	B	B	C	A	B	C	B	B	–	–	–	–	–	–	–
118	B	B	B	A	A	C	B	B	A	C	A	A	C	B	A
119	B	B	B	A	A	E	A	A	A	AC	AB	B	A	E	B
120	E	B	D	A	A	C	A	A	–	–	–	–	–	–	–
121	B	B	B	B	A	A	D	B	A	C	A	B	C	A	A
122	B	B	F	A	A	A	F	A	–	–	–	–	–	–	–
123	C	A	A	B	A	C	E	B	A	–	–	–	–	–	–
124	A	A	A	A	A	C	C	A	A	AC	ABI	B	C	B	A
125	B	A	C	A	A	C	C	A	A	AC	AB	B	C	D	A
126	B	B	C	A	A	C	A	A	A	–	–	–	–	–	–

50

LESS
3%

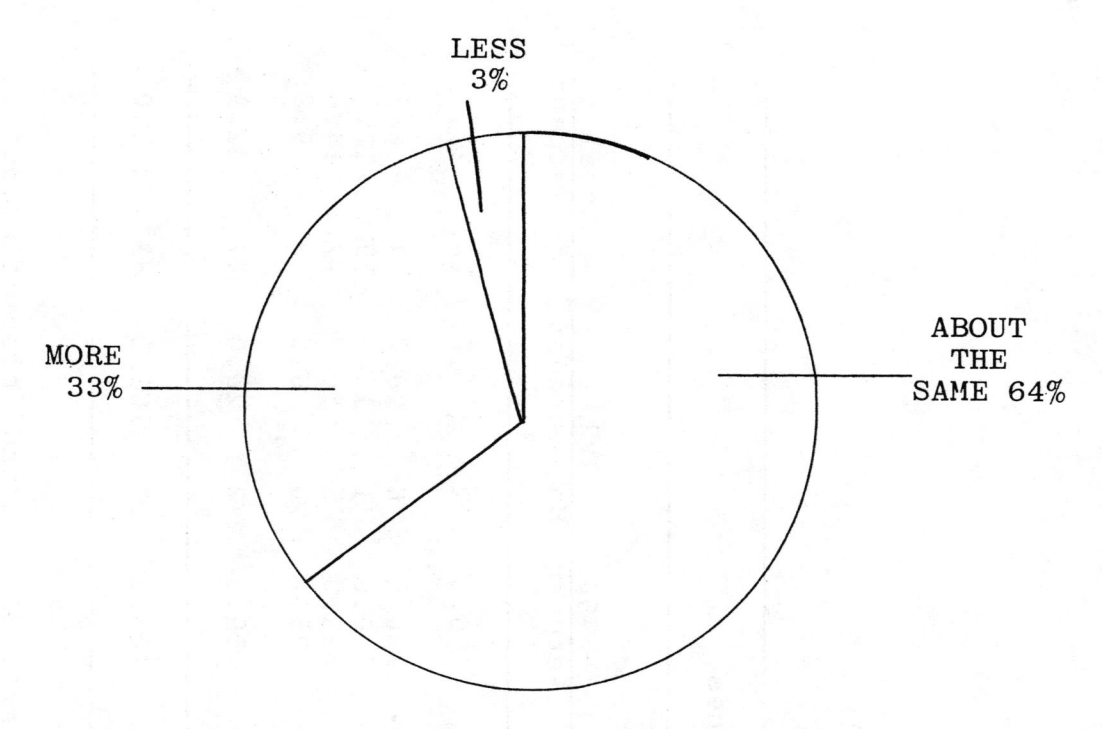

MORE
33%

ABOUT
THE
SAME 64%

Figure (No.).   (Fill in appropriate title.)

(The above pie chart shows responses to question 13 on sample questionnaire to be used with Lab VI.)

TABLE (NO.)

(APPROPRIATE TITLE)

Monthly Income	Less Than $100 No.	Less Than $100 Percent	$100-$200 No.	$100-$200 Percent	$201-$300 No.	$201-$300 Percent	$301-$400 No.	$301-$400 Percent	Other No.	Other Percent	Total No.	Total Percent
0	12	25.5	4	23.5	0	0.0	0	0.0	2	0.0	18	22.0
Less Than $100	4	8.5	3	17.7	0	0.0	0	0.0	0	0.0	7	8.5
$101-$200	8	17.0	1	5.9	0	0.0	0	0.0	1	10.0	10	12.1
$201-$300	5	10.6	0	0.0	1	25.0	1	25.0	5	50.0	12	14.6
$301-$400	4	8.5	2	11.8	1	25.0	1	25.0	0	0.0	8	9.8
More Than $400	14	29.9	7	41.1	2	50.0	2	50.0	2	20.0	27	32.9
Totals	97	100.0	17	100.0	4	100.0	4	100.0	10	100.0	82[a]	100.0

Total Charges

[a] Of the 100 students surveyed who possessed credit cards, 82 returned information as to their total charges.

(This table shows responses to questions 7 and 15 on sample questionnaire to be used with Lab VI.)

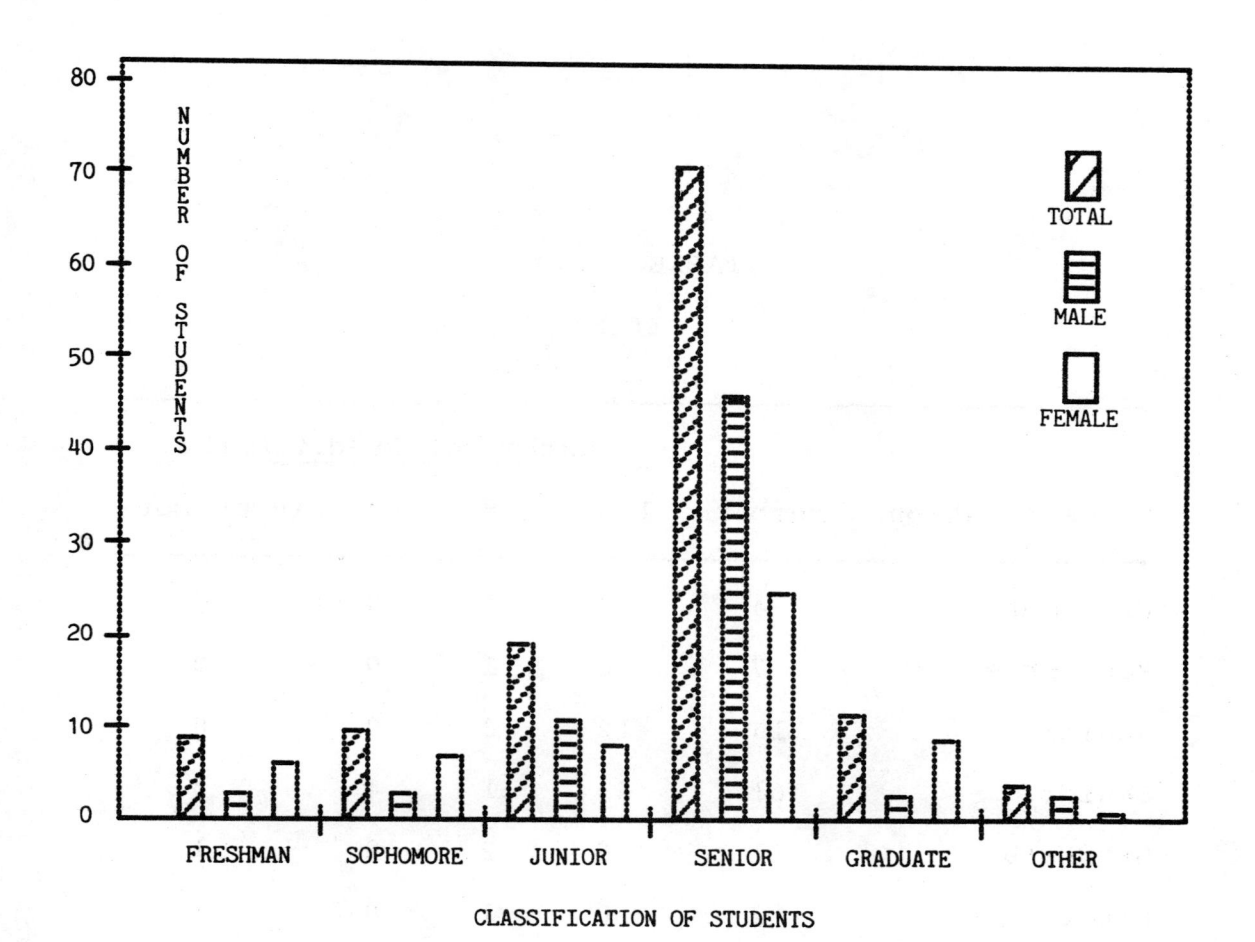

Figure (No.). (Fill in appropriate title.)

(The above comparison bar chart shows responses to questions 2 and 3 on sample questionnaire to be used with Lab VI.)

TABLE (NO.)

(TITLE)

| | | Number of Credit Cards | | | |
Classification	Number	1-3	4-8	7-9	10 or More
Freshman	4	3	1	0	0
Sophomore	7	6	1	0	0
Junior	15	12	3	0	0
Senior	61	43	11	4	3
Graduate	11	6	2	0	1
Other	2	0	1	0	1
Totals	100	70	19	6	5

(The above table shows responses to questions 3 and 9 on sample questionnaire.)

NO
20%

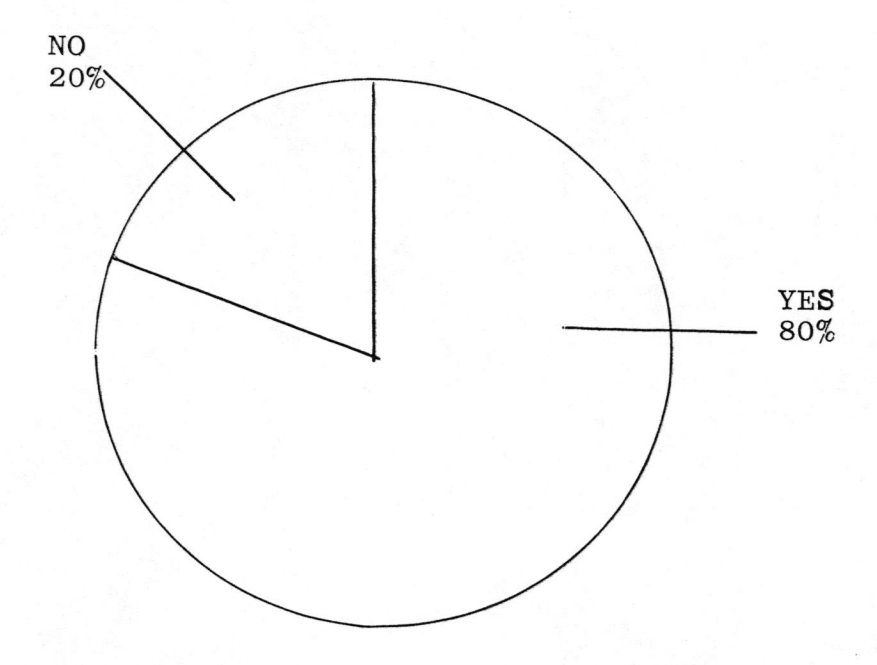

YES
80%

Figure (No.). (Fill in appropriate title.)

(The above pie chart shows responses to question 8 on sample questionnaire to be used with Lab VI.)

LAB VII

EVALUATION II

Objectives

To interpret the primary data collected.

To use and construct tables, charts, and graphs and integrate them with the text.

Instructions

1. Open a document on your data disk using the name **EVAL2**.

2. Type the Interpretation of the Data compiled from the responses to the questionnaire developed for your **final** report.

3. **SAVE** the document.

4. Open a document on your data disk using the name **EVAL2.1**.

5. Merge document named **EVAL1**.

6. Merge document named **EVAL2**.

7. **SAVE** the document.

8. **PRINT** the document.

9. Turn in the printed document.

Assignment for Lab VIII

1. Review lecture notes and textbook assignments on stating findings, deriving conclusions, and making recommendations.

2. Review lecture notes and textbook assignments on preparing prefatory and supplemental pages for a report.

3. Be prepared to type the findings, conclusions, and recommendations for your **practice** report.

4. Be prepared to type the supplemental pages for you **practice** report.

LAB VIII

ACTIVITIES 11-14

Objectives

To state the findings, derive conclusions, and make recommendations.

To prepare the prefatory and supplemental pages of the report.

To write an analytical report.

Concept(s) Prerequisite to Lab VII

1. Stating the Findings

2. Deriving Conclusions

3. Making Recommendations

ACTIVITY 11

Instructions

1. Open a document named **ACT11**. Be sure to indicate that you will be working on your data disk.

2. State the findings discussed in the data interpretation.

3. State the conclusions derived. They should be based on the findings.

4. If recommendations are made, they should evolve naturally from the conclusions derived.

5. **SAVE** the document.

6. **PRINT** the document.

ACTIVITY 12

Instructions

1. Open a document using the name **ACT12**.
2. Prepare the title page.
3. Write a letter of transmittal. It should
   a. carry a warm greeting to the reader
   b. open quickly with, "Here is the report you requested . . ."
   c. establish the subject in the first sentence
   d. give a brief summary of the report
   e. close with a "thank you."
4. Prepare a Table of Contents.
5. Prepare a List of Tables.
6. Prepare a List of Figures.
7. Merge **ACT8**.
8. **SAVE** the document.

ACTIVITY 13

Instructions

1. Open a document on your data disk using the name **ACT13**.

2. Prepare the bibliography.

3. Prepare the appendices divider page.

4. **SAVE** the document.

ACTIVITY 14

Instructions

1. Open a document on your data disk using the name **ACT14**.

2. Merge **ACT12**.

3. Merge **ACT10.1**.

4. Merge **ACT13**.

5. **SAVE** the document.

6. **PRINT** the document.

7. Turn in the completed report. Include all tables, charts, and graphs and the appendices in the appropriate places.

Assignment for Lab IX

Lab IX will be your third evaluation lab and will represent an important part of your final grade. You should

1. Review your lecture notes and textbook assignments on the concepts covered to this point.

2. Be prepared to type your findings, conclusions, and recommendations for your **final** report.

3. Be prepared to type the prefatory and supplemental pages for your **final** report.

LAB IX

EVALUATION III

Objectives

To state the findings, derive conclusions, and make recommendations.

To prepare the prefatory and supplemental parts.

To merge and print all components of the analytical report.

Instructions

1. Open a document on your data disk using the name **EVAL3**.

2. Type the findings, conclusions, and recommendations.

3. **SAVE** the document.

4. Open a document on your data disk using the name **EVAL3.1**.

5. Type the prefatory parts:

    a. Title Page
    b. Letter of Transmittal
    c. Table of Contents
    d. List of Tables
    e. List of Figures

6. **SAVE** the document.

7. Open a document on your data disk using the name **EVAL3.2**.

8. Type the supplemental pages:

    a. Bibliography
    b. Appendices divider page

9. **SAVE** the document.

10. Merge documents **EVAL3.1**, **EVAL2.1**, **EVAL3**, and **EVAL3.2**.

11. **SAVE** the document.

12. **PRINT** the document.

13. Turn in the completed **final** report.

Assignment for Lab X

1. Review lecture notes and textbook assignments on writing letter reports.

2. Be prepared to write a letter report to the president of the local Chamber of Commerce. He has heard about the research project you have been working on related to the effects of credit card usage on college students. He would like to present the findings of this report at a meeting of the Chamber of Commerce.

LAB X

ACTIVITY 15

Objective(s)

To write a letter report.

Concept(s) Prerequisite to Lab X

1. Identifying the Reader
2. Presenting Background Information
3. Identifying Procedures and Sources of Data
4. Summarizing the Findings
5. Letter Report Format

Instructions

1. Open a document on your data disk using the name **ACT15**.

2. The president of the local Chamber of Commerce has learned of your research project on the effects of credit card usage by university students. He is interested in presenting the findings of your study at a meeting of the Chamber of Commerce and has requested this information.

3. Write a letter report to the president of the local Chamber of Commerce providing him with the following information:

    a. a reference to his request
    b. background information about the research project
    c. nature of research
    d. summary of the tentative findings
    e. an expression of thanks for his interest in your research project.

4. **SAVE** your document.

5. **PRINT** the document.

6. Turn in the printed document.

REFERENCE GUIDE

REFERENCE GUIDE

Study your software applications package and complete the following matrix to use as a reference as needed while you complete the laboratory activities. In the right-hand column identify the steps necessary to perform the function listed in the left-hand column.

The following is given as an example. The function will be repeated so that you can complete it for use with your software.

Getting Started:

    LOAD SOFTWARE   Turn on the system.

                                   Insert word processing disk in drive __A__ and close the disk drive door.

                                   Insert data disk in drive __B__ and close the disk drive door.

                                   Press _____RESET_____.

                                   The Directory Menu will appear on your screen.

TYPING AND SAVING FILES

Getting Started:

    LOAD SOFTWARE

Typing a Document:

    OPEN A DOCUMENT

Saving Your Work:

    SAVE DOCUMENT AND
    DISPLAY DIRECTORY
    MENU

    SAVE DOCUMENT AND
    REDISPLAY DOCUMENT

SETTING MARGINS, TABS, AND LINE SPACING

Margins:

    CHANGE LEFT MARGIN

    CHANGE RIGHT MARGIN

Tabs:

    CLEAR ONE TAB

    CLEAR ALL TABS

    SET TAB

    SET DECIMAL (ALIGN) TAB

    AUTOMATIC INDENT TAB

Line Spacing:

    SET LINE SPACING

    CHANGE LINE SPACING

PRINTING AND WORKING WITH BLOCKS

<u>Printing</u>:

    PRINT A DOCUMENT
    FROM DIRECTORY

    PRINT FROM AN
    OPEN DOCUMENT

<u>Working With Blocks</u>:

    MARK BLOCK BEGINNING

    MARK BLOCK ENDING

    COPY BLOCK

    MOVE BLOCK

    COPY BLOCK TO
    ANOTHER DOCUMENT

DELETE BLOCK

OVERSTRIKE AND SUB/SUPERSCRIPT

<u>Overstrike</u>:

    START OVERSTRIKE

    STOP OVERSTRIKE

<u>Sub and Superscripts</u>:

    START SUBSCRIPT

    STOP SUBSCRIPT

    START SUPERSCRIPT

    STOP SUPERSCRIPT

BOLDING, CENTERING, AND UNDERSCORING

<u>Bolding</u>:

    START BOLDING

    STOP BOLDING

<u>Centering</u>:

    CENTER

<u>Underscoring</u>:

    START UNDERSCORING

    STOP UNDERSCORING

INSERTING TEXT

<u>Inserting</u>:

    TEXT WITHIN A
    PARAGRAPH

A NEW PARAGRAPH

MISCELLANEOUS FUNCTIONS

REQUIRED PAGE BREAK

USING HEADERS ON PAGE

USING FOOTERS ON PAGE

NUMBERING PAGES AUTOMATICALLY

OMITTING PAGE NUMBERS

REFORMATTING A DOCUMENT

MERGING DOCUMENTS

CHECKING SPACE
ON DISK IN
DRIVE A (0)

CHECKING SPACE
ON DISK IN
DRIVE B (1)

HYPHENATING TO MAKE
LINE ENDINGS MORE
ATTRACTIVE

RETRIEVING A STORED
DOCUMENT

Identify the Standard Format Settings for your software:

    MARGINS

    TABS

    LINE SPACING

    JUSTIFICATION

    TOP AND BOTTOM
    MARGINS

    PAPER LENGTH